By Deborah Chancellor
Designed by Liz Black
Cover design by Robert Perry

KINGFISHER BOOKS
An imprint of Larousse plc
New Penderel House
238-288 High Holborn
London WC1V 7HZ

First published by Larousse plc 1996

4 6 8 10 9 7 5 3

A CIP catalogue record for this book is available from the British Library

ISBN 0 7534 0082 0

KINGfISHER

BUT BILLY'S HIGH SPEED FEET HAVE A STRANGE EFFECT AND UP IN SPACE —

BILLY, YOUR JOGGING HAS STARTED THE WORLD SPINNING BACKWARDS. IF YOU DON'T STOP NOW, TIME WILL HAVE BEEN REVERSED AND WE'LL ALL END UP IN THE PAST.

OH-OH! TOO LATE!
SCREECH!

TO BE MORE ACCURATE . . . TOO EARLY!

DINOSAUR DETECTIVES

FOLLOWING CLUES

Dinosaurs left big clues behind in the shape of fossils. Whole skeletons have been discovered buried deep in rock. It takes a lot of hard work to get them out.

Dinosaurs were some of the most exciting animals in the history of the world. But the last dinosaurs died out 65 million years ago, so how do we know about these amazing creatures?

THE DINOSAUR AGE

Dinosaurs roamed the Earth for about 160 million years. It is hard to imagine such an enormous length of time – we human beings have only been around for about the last two million years!

One of the first jobs the scientists do is to make a map of the area.

The last 20 centimetres above the dinosaur are chipped away by hand.

The site is drawn and photographed before any of the bones are dug out.

The bones are covered with plaster to protect them before they are removed from the site.

HOW ARE FOSSILS DATED?

Scientists can calculate how old a fossil is by working out the age of the surrounding rock it has been found in.

HOW FOSSILS ARE MADE

This process takes millions of years!

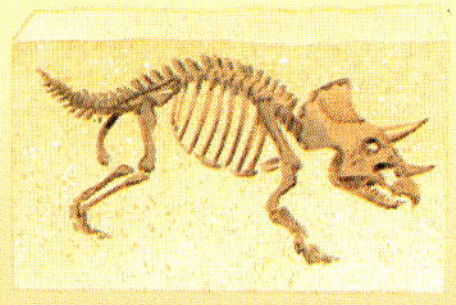

- ***Mud and sand cover a dead dinosaur.***
- ***The mud and sand turn to rock, and minerals fill the dinosaur bones.***

- ***Movements in the earth gradually break up the skeleton.***
- ***Wind and rain wear away the rock and expose the fossil.***

GUESS WORK

We can also guess what dinosaurs were like by looking at animals today. Perhaps some dinosaurs were camouflaged to hide from enemies, or brightly coloured to help them warn off predators.

THE FIRST DINOSAURS

There were many different kinds of dinosaur, but they didn't all live at the same time. The first dinosaurs appeared about 230 million years ago in a period of time known as the Triassic Period.

Coelophysis

WHEN DID DINOSAURS FIRST ROAM THE EARTH?

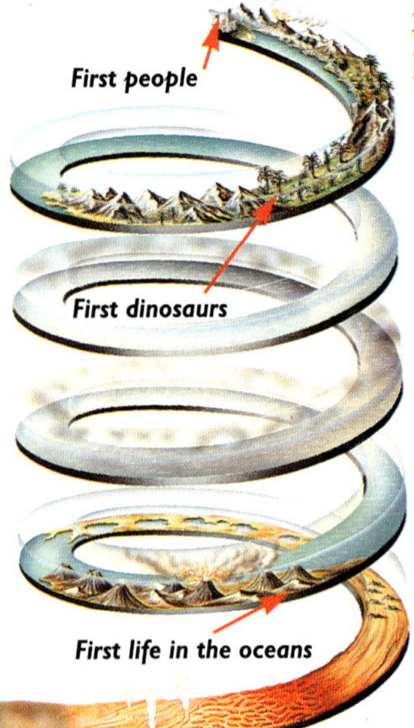

Dinosaurs first walked the Earth many millions of years before human beings arrived.

Conifers

THE TRIASSIC WORLD

The world looked very different in the Triassic Period, with dry deserts inland and lush green areas near coasts and rivers. There were no flowers, and typical Triassic plants included conifers, ferns and cycads.

Cycads

SMALL BEGINNINGS

The average Triassic dinosaur was only about as tall as a human adult!

IT'S THE FIRST CREATURE TO CRAWL ON TO DRY LAND!

- Coelophysis was a small Triassic meat-eater. Tyrannosaurus rex evolved from this type of dinosaur.

Plateosaurus

- Plateosaurus was one of the very first long-necked dinosaurs. At eight metres long, it was ten times smaller than Diplodocus.

- Lesothosaurus was a tiny Triassic plant-eater. This dinosaur midget was only 90 cm from tip to tail.

WHAT CAME BEFORE THE DINOSAURS?

Life on Earth began in the water. About 300 million years before the arrival of the first dinosaurs, there was a gradual move away from water on to dry land. Creatures called amphibians spent some time on land, but still depended on water to survive and lay their eggs. Reptiles then evolved, living and laying eggs on the land. Dinosaurs developed from these early reptiles.

RISE OF THE DINOSAURS

The middle part of the dinosaur age was called the Jurassic Period. It began about 200 million years ago and lasted 60 million years. During this time, dinosaurs gradually got bigger and bigger. Huge long-necked giants and terrifying meat-eaters dominated the Jurassic landscape.

THE JURASSIC WORLD

The Jurassic world was much cooler than the Triassic and there was a more definite pattern of seasons.

Many different types of dinosaur emerged in the Jurassic period, and it is often called the 'Age of Dinosaurs'.

LIFE ON A LARGE SCALE

Typical animals of the Jurassic were giants compared to modern animals. Today, the African elephant is the world's biggest land animal alive. The largest dinosaur however, was ten times bigger than this!

BIG FRIGHT

Allosaurus was a typical Jurassic carnivore. Measuring over ten metres long, this frightening beast preyed on smaller dinosaurs, such as Stegosaurus. Its great jaws were lined with over 70 razor-sharp teeth.

BIG APPETITES

The massive dinosaurs with long necks and tails are called sauropods. There must have been a lot of vegetation about in the Triassic period, because each sauropod could munch through up to 100 kilograms of plant material a day!

NECK ACHE

Why do you think that the Jurassic sauropods had such long necks?

- To feed on one spot and save energy?
- To wallow in deep water?
- To feed on the tree tops?

The truth is, no one really knows the right answer.

THE LAST DINOSAURS

The last stage of dinosaur history is called the Cretaceous Period. During these 75 million years, some of the strangest and most spectacular looking dinosaurs evolved. The world around them also changed to become much more like the environment we know today.

Spinosaurus

THE CRETACEOUS WORLD

Flowers began to bloom in the Cretaceous Period, bringing colour to the dinosaurs' world. Butterflies and bees collected pollen from the new plants. Fruit and vegetables appeared, giving the dinosaurs a much greater choice of food.

SPIKES AND FRILLS

Triceratops is one of the most famous Cretaceous dinosaurs, with three sharp horns on its head and a bony neck frill. This peaceful plant-eater probably looked like this to warn other fierce meat-eating dinosaurs not to attack them.

HARD HEADS

Pachycephalosaurus was lucky enough to have a built-in crash helmet! The top of its head was a thick bony dome, strong enough to take a head-on collision. It may have had head-butting contests to win a mate, or to decide who should be the leader of the herd. Pachycephalosaurus was 4.5 metres long – the biggest of the 'bone head' group of dinosaurs.

DEATH OF THE DINOSAURS

There were an amazing five million generations of dinosaurs, but something happened to end the family line. No one knows exactly what killed off the dinosaurs and many other animals that were around at the time, but there are lots of fantastic theories.

BLAST FROM SPACE

Perhaps an asteroid crashed into the Earth from outer space, making a massive dust cloud which blocked out the Sun's light. The temperature then dropped to below freezing and acid rain fell. Scientists have found a huge crater in Central America, which could be where the asteroid landed.

WHAT REALLY HAPPENED?

There are many more theories to explain the death of the dinosaurs. Here are just a few:

- New plants poisoned the dinosaurs
- Mammals ate all the dinosaur eggs
- Volcanic eruptions caused global warming
- The climate became too cold for the dinosaurs

THE SURVIVORS

Mammals were small and shrew-like during the reign of the dinosaurs. After the big wipe-out, they slowly evolved to take over as the world's most powerful creatures. Birds, reptiles and amphibians also survived, and are still with us today.

ANCIENT GIANTS

The long-necked dinosaurs were the biggest animals that ever walked the Earth. They grew so large in order to protect themselves from their fierce enemies – it was hard to kill such enormous beasts. Being so big and tall also meant the gentle giants could spot danger from a long way off.

IT'S A LONG TAIL

Diplodocus was the longest dinosaur, stretching out to an amazing 27 m. Much of this length was taken up by its long tail. Yet it was light for its length – Diplodocus only weighed 11 tonnes!

Diplodocus defending itself with its tail

TALL STORY

Let's hope that the Mamenchisaurus never got a sore throat! This dinosaur's neck was 15 m long – six times longer than a giraffe's. Perhaps it stood in a lake so its neck could float in the water. It could have eaten lakeside plants, sucking them up like a monster-sized vacuum cleaner.

HEAVYWEIGHT CHAMP

Imagine ten elephants treading on your toes! Brachiosaurus was as heavy as this, and at over 70 tonnes, it was the weightiest creature the world has ever seen. Standing 12 m tall and 22 m long, Brachiosaurus lived on a vegetarian diet.

***Brachiosaurus* herd**

Mamenchisaurus

IT WASN'T ALL DANGER WITH THE DINOSAURS!

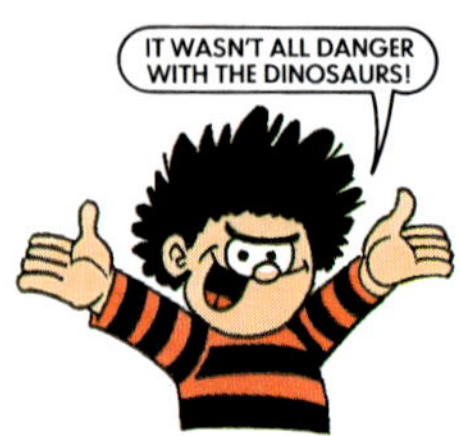

LARGEST OF ALL

Scientists are now sure that an even bigger sauropod lived in Jurassic times. They have discovered the bones of a dinosaur called Seismosaurus that was over 70 m long!

HOW DID THEY MOVE?

- These dinosaurs had long legs like thick pillars to support their huge weight.
- The tail balanced the neck, and was probably held above the ground.
- Two feet were always kept on the ground, so no running or jumping!

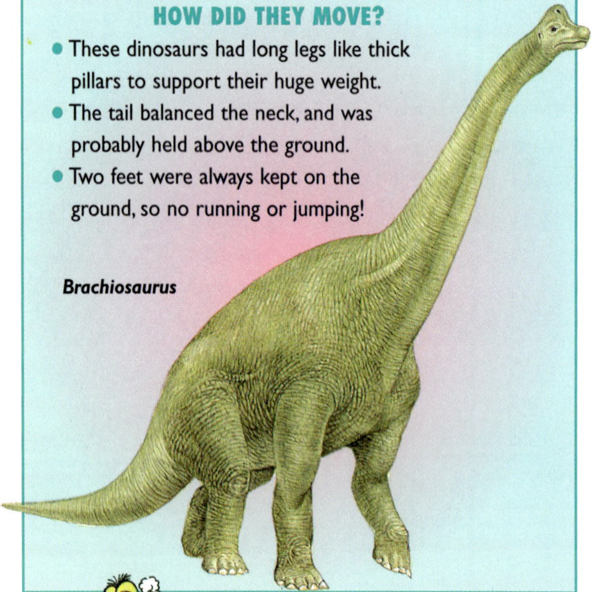

Brachiosaurus

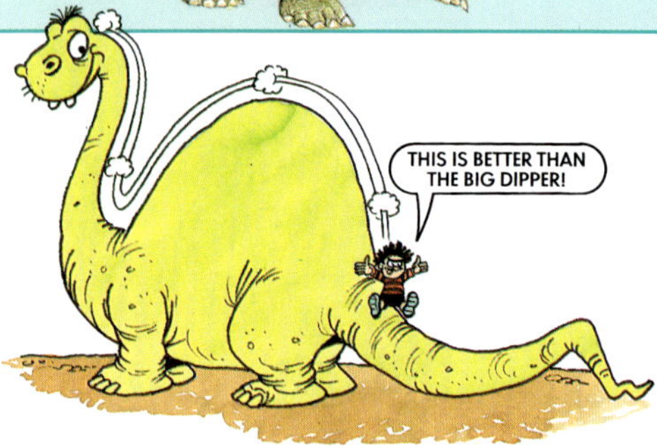
THIS IS BETTER THAN THE BIG DIPPER!

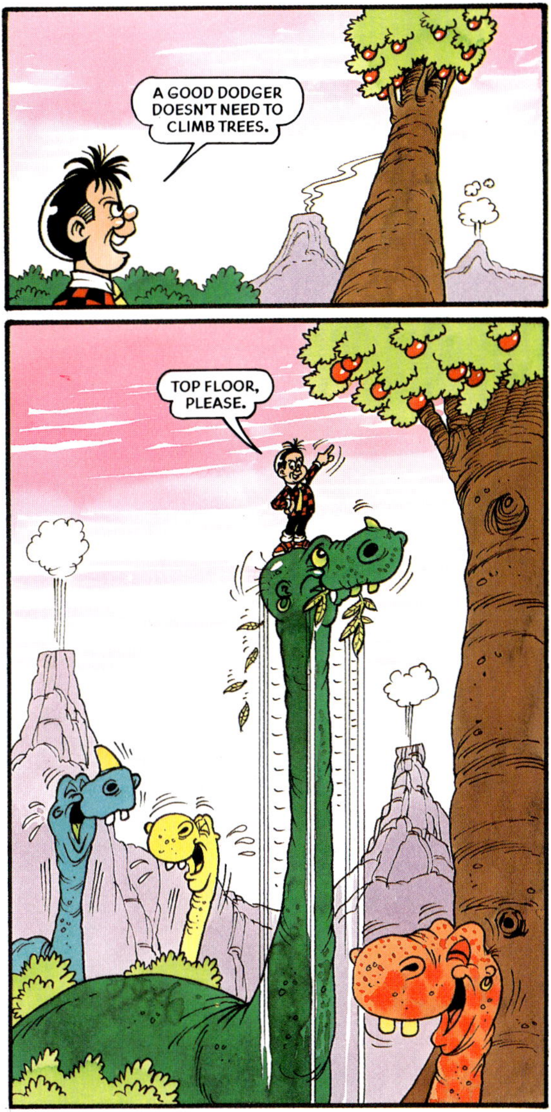

TOP FLOOR, PLEASE.

THE MIDGETS

Compsognathus

Dinosaurs came in many different shapes and sizes – not all of them were enormous! Some were tiny, which meant they were faster and much more agile than the lumbering giant sauropods.

TINY TERROR

Compsognathus was the smallest dinosaur of them all. This midget was only about the size of a chicken. Even though it could reach up to 70 cm in length, more than half of this this was taken up by its flashing tail. What Compsognathus lacked in size, it made up for in speed. Strong back legs were built for fast dashes, both away from danger and after food. 'Compsognathus' means 'pretty jaw', but this little nipper probably had a very nasty bite indeed!

SMALL START

Protoceratops was a small relative of the much larger dinosaur Triceratops. Protoceratops babies were only 30 cm long, but they grew up to two metres from head to foot. A neck frill gave some protection from attack, but unlike Triceratops, this dinosaur did not have sharp horns to scare off its enemies.

MINI HUNTER

Coelophysis was another small but active hunter. From head to tail, Coelophysis was three metres long, and could stand upright on its back legs, ready to sprint after prey. Its front legs were probably used to rip at its food, just as birds of prey do today.

Coelophysis

BRAIN BOXES

IF YOU'RE SO CLEVER, DO MY HOMEWORK!

MAYBE YOU'RE NOT SO DAFT!

Some people think all dinosaurs were clumsy and stupid – but this just wasn't true. Many dinosaurs were actually quite intelligent, with big brains in relation to the size of their bodies.

TOP OF THE CLASS

Stenonychosaurus was one of the brainiest dinosaurs, with a bigger brain than that of a modern reptile. It had excellent eyesight and a good sense of balance. This nimble hunter probably chased small animals after dark.

Stenonychosaurus

THE CHAMP

Struthiomimus ran faster than any animal alive today. At 50 km per hour, it raced at twice the speed of a human sprinter! It had a big brain, which it used to coordinate its movements. The skeleton of Struthiomimus is just like an ostrich skeleton, so the dinosaur probably looked like a large scaly ostrich, with skinny arms and a long tail.

Struthiomimus

THE DUNCE

Stegosaurus was no genius! This 1.5 tonne dinosaur had a brain the size of a walnut – a 1.5 tonne elephant has a brain 30 times bigger than this! One brain wasn't enough for Stegosaurus – it needed a second brain behind its back legs to control its tail. Stegosaurus had a simple life grazing on plants, so it didn't need too much brain power anyway!

Stegosaurus

GREEDY GUTS

Dinosaurs enjoyed eating many different kinds of food. Some browsed on plants, while others ate the flesh of anything meaty enough to hunt. A few dinosaurs even caught fish. You can often guess what kind of food a dinosaur ate by looking at the type of teeth and the shape of its mouth.

Iguanodon

Iguanodon tooth (5 cm long)

CHEWY CHOPS

Iguanodon had a mouth shaped like a bony beak, full of big ridged teeth for grinding down plants. It had large cheeks for chewing leafy mouthfuls.

FISHY FEAST

Baryonyx had jaws like a crocodile's. This nine-metre long dinosaur probably speared fish with its hooked claws, snapped them up in its jaws and then crunched the bones with its razor-sharp teeth. A skeleton of Baryonyx has been found with fish scales in the stomach – this is probably the remains of the dinosaur's last meal.

Baryonyx

MEATY MOUTHS

Many dinosaurs were meat-eaters, or carnivores. One particularly fierce hunter of the Jurassic Period was Ceratosaurus. It had massive, sharp fangs in its strong jaws for tearing into meat. It had a horn on its nose – a very useful weapon in a fight!

CANNIBAL!

Inside the stomach of Coelophysis, scientists found the bones of a younger dinosaur of the same species. It was far too big to be an unborn baby, so Coelophysis was probably a cannibal.

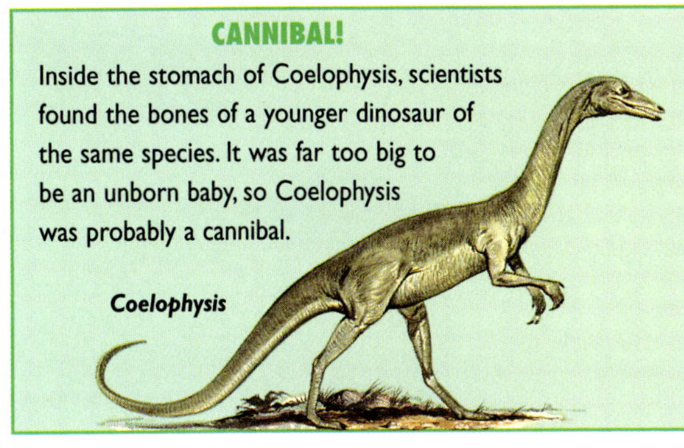

Coelophysis

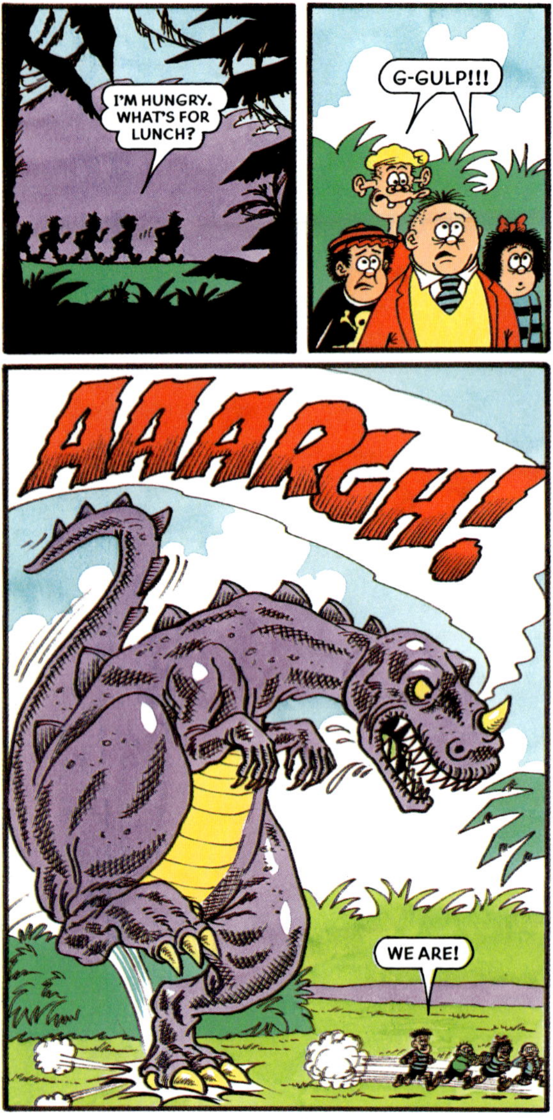

AAARGH!

WE ARE!

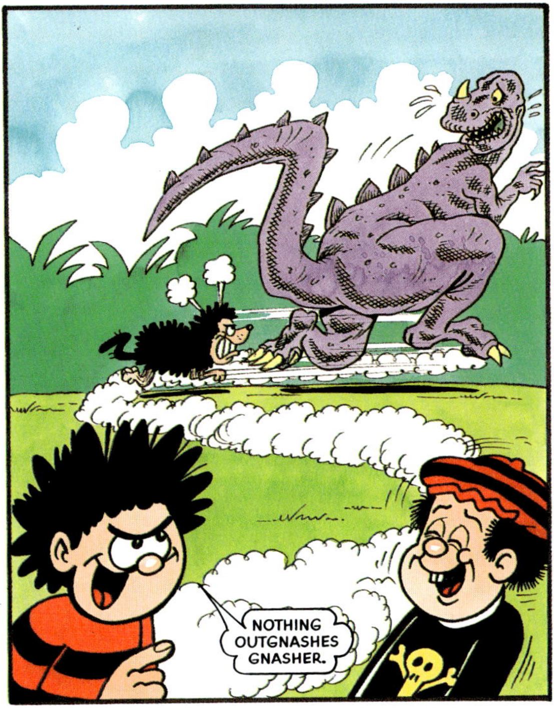

NOTHING OUTGNASHES GNASHER.

THE BULLIES

Tyrannosaurus rex

The world of the dinosaurs must have been a very dangerous place – it's a good job we weren't around at the time to see for ourselves! Powerful meat-eaters prowled the Earth in search of prey, hunting as often as they were hungry. Dinosaurs were some of the biggest bullies that ever lived.

DEADLY BITE

If Tyrannosaurus rex were alive today, it could probably swallow a human being whole. A five-year-old could stand up in its gaping jaws, but that wouldn't be a good idea! Its metre-long mouth was crammed with teeth as big and sharp as butcher's knives.

BULLY OR COWARD?

Tyrannosaurus had very small spindly arms – they couldn't even reach its huge mouth! So it may not have been a good hunter. Perhaps it survived by scaring other dinosaurs off their meal, and then gobbling up the left-overs.

SPINE CHILLER

Spinosaurus was a dangerous Cretaceous hunter. It had strange looks, with a big 'sail' along its spine which must have frightened its prey. This 15 m long dinosaur was the biggest of the meat-eating group called the carnosaurs.

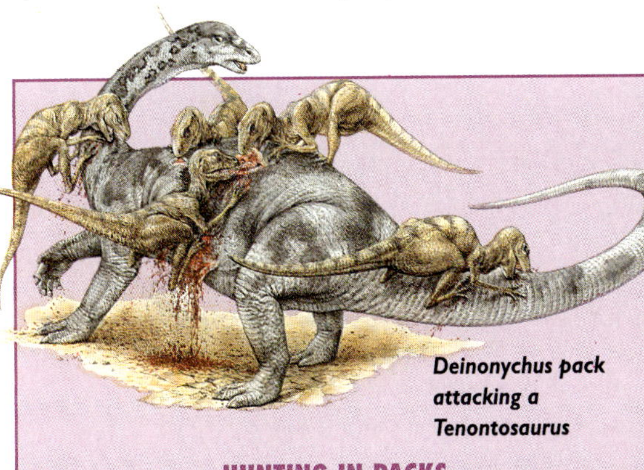

Deinonychus pack attacking a Tenontosaurus

HUNTING IN PACKS

Small dinosaurs were often much more dangerous than their larger, plant-eating relatives. They combined speed with intelligence to track down prey, and were armed with deadly teeth and sharp claws for the kill. Deinonychus and Velociraptor hunted in packs, like lions do today.

FIGHTING BACK

The big bullies of the dinosaur age didn't have everything their own way. The dinosaurs they hunted developed good ways of fighting back, or avoiding an attack altogether.

BRAVE TAILS

Diplodocus

Tails were not just to help with balance – sometimes they were useful weapons in the fight against bullies.

- Diplodocus swished its long thin tail about like a whip, knocking other dinosaurs off their feet.
- Stegosaurus had sharp spikes on the end of its tail, which it could swing in the face of an enemy.

Stegosaurus

GOING CLUBBING

Ankylosaurus was a Cretaceous dinosaur that was built like a tank. Its 11 m long body was covered with spines and bone plates. If Ankylosaurus ever had to fight, it would swing its tail from side to side – the bony club at the end could cause a serious injury.

QUICK GETAWAY

For some dinosaurs the only way of escaping attack was to run away! Gallimimus was a graceful athlete, and could run as fast as a racehorse. Its tail stretched out like a stiff rod to help it balance at top speeds.

SAFETY IN NUMBERS

Just like many animals today, some dinosaurs lived together in herds. We know this because big family groups have been found, for example 39 Iguanodon skeletons were discovered down a mine in Belgium. This herd was probably killed by a natural disaster, such as a landslide.

WATCH OUT!

The main reason for living in a group was that it was safer, and some members of the herd could always watch out for danger. Parasaurolophus had a fancy head crest, which wasn't just for show. The duck-billed dinosaur made trumpet noises with its crest to warn the herd of an attack.

The tubes inside the crest of Parasaurolophus were attached to its nostrils, so it could hoot and chew at the same time.

LIVING IN A GROUP

Corythosaurus was another crested dinosaur that lived in a herd. The colourful crest was probably used for attracting a mate and recognizing other dinosaurs of the same species.

Diplodocus herd

BABIES ON BOARD

Diplodocus was so huge, it was probaby hard to attack, but its babies weren't so safe. When a Diplocodus herd was on the move, the young walked in the middle, protected on all sides by the adults.

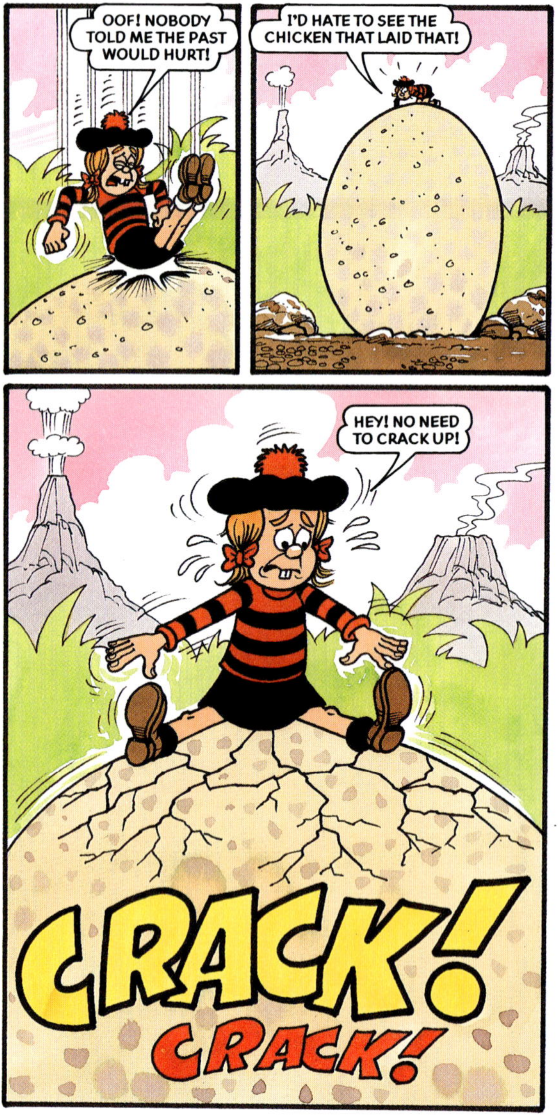

HEY! NO NEED TO CRACK UP!

CRACK!

CRACK!

WOW!

I WONDER IF
DAD WILL LET
ME KEEP HIM.

DINOSAUR BABIES

It is hard to imagine a large dinosaur laying an egg, but that is how dinosaur babies came into the world. Dinosaur eggs were quite small – if they were too big, the baby wouldn't be able to break its way out of the thick shell.

I LOVE EGG PAINTING!

LOOK INSIDE

Scientists now use special equipment to look inside dinosaur eggs, millions of years after they were first laid!

GROWING UP

Maiasaura babies were only 35 cm long when they hatched – a hundred times smaller than their parents! Their mothers looked after them in the nest, bringing food and keeping them warm, until they grew to about a metre long. Then they joined the family herd, growing to three metres by their first birthday.

Maiasaura and babies

NOT SO BIG

It is surprising that the biggest dinosaur eggs found so far are only five times bigger than a hen's egg.

EGG THIEF

Tasty eggs were a big temptation for Oviraptor, whose name literally means 'egg thief'. We know this because an Oviraptor skeleton has been found at a Protoceratops nest site. Oviraptor probably held eggs in its long, grasping fingers, and cracked them open in its strong, curved jaws.

LEAVING THE NEST

Hypsilophodon eggs were laid in warm sand in a spiral pattern. The babies left the nest as soon as they hatched – we know this because lots of broken shells have been found at nest sites, but few baby skeletons.

PROTECTIVE PARENTS

Although it was a peaceful plant-eater, Triceratops' survival depended on its great neck frill and sharp horns! During their first few months of life, young Triceratops relied on their fierce-looking parents to protect them from passing meat-eaters.

Triceratops and young

MONSTERS OF THE DEEP

Some dinosaurs could probably swim, but they didn't live in the water. The prehistoric seas were full of other weird and wonderful reptiles. Some were better adapted to life at sea than others.

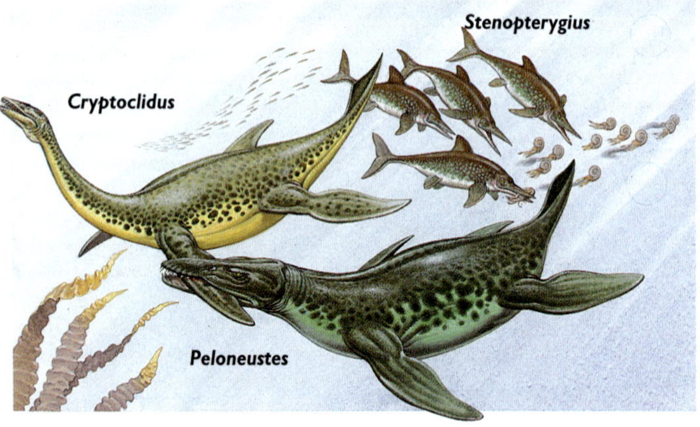

EARLY SWIMMERS

The biggest group of sea reptiles during the Triassic Period were animals with four flippers called Plesiosaurs. We know a lot about these creatures from the fossil remains they have left behind. Cryptoclidus was a huge long-necked creature that hunted fish. Its jaws were packed with sharp teeth which were perfect for snapping up its prey. Peloneustes had a whale-shaped body and a thick, short neck.

LIFE AT SEA

Jurassic and Cretaceous swimmers were more adventurous. Plesiosauroids flapped large flippers to 'fly' under water. Like dinosaurs, these long-necked creatures sometimes grew to immense sizes. Elasmosaurus was an incredible 14 m long!

SCARY MONSTERS

Pliosauroids had short necks and big powerful jaws, lined with sharp, bone-crunching teeth. Kronosaurus was the biggest of them all, and its head alone measured almost three metres in length.

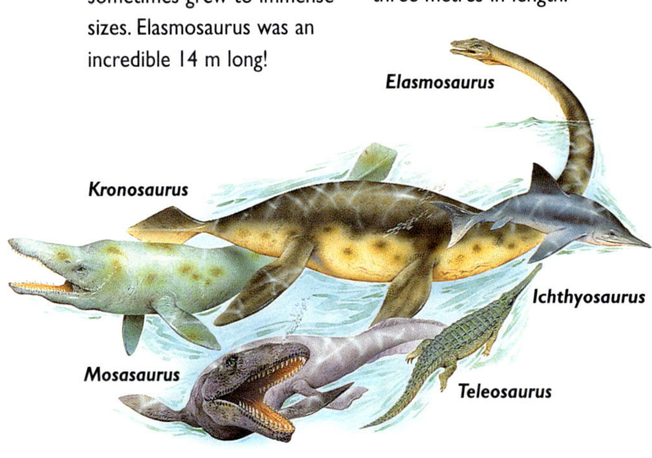

SEA CROCODILES

Crocodiles swam in the sea during the dinosaur age. Just like crocodiles today, their long jaws were lined with jagged teeth. Teleosaurus had an especially long, thin snout.

BORN TO SWIM

Ichthyosaurs were the best swimmers of the Cretaceous Period. These water-loving reptiles had graceful streamlined bodies like dolphins, but they swam more like sharks, flicking their powerful tails from side to side. Some reached tremendous speeds of up to 40 km per hour.

Ichthyosaurus

SEA BABIES

Unlike many other ocean going reptiles, Ichthyosaurs didn't need to drag themselves on to land to lay eggs. They gave birth underwater, just like whales do today

TURTLE POWER

Ichthyosaurs and many other swimming reptiles died out with the dinosaurs. For some reason, turtles survived, and are still swimming the seas today. Some Cretaceous turtles were enormous – Archelon was 3.75 m long, the size of a large rowing boat!

GIANT LIZARDS

As well as sea reptiles, enormous lizards also took to the prehistoric oceans. Mosasaurus had paddles for legs and fins on its tail. This sea monster measured over ten metres long! It had a long slender body and a deep flat-sided tail which it used to propel itself through the water. At the end of the Cretaceous period, Mosasaurs took over from Ichthyosaurs as the main sea hunters.

Opthalamosaurus shoal

WHAT BIG EYES YOU'VE GOT

Ichthyosaurs hunted fish and squid, so they needed sharp eyesight to spot their darting underwater prey. Opthalamosaurus had eyes which were 19 cm in diameter – as big as dinner plates!

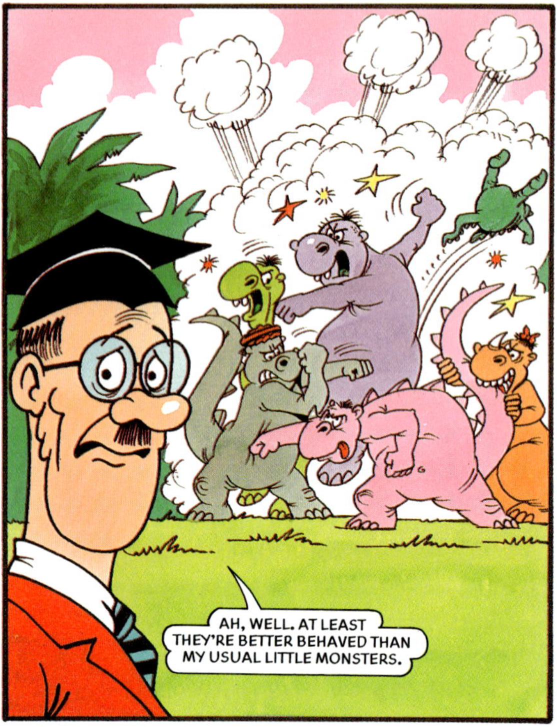

AH, WELL. AT LEAST THEY'RE BETTER BEHAVED THAN MY USUAL LITTLE MONSTERS.

KINGS OF THE AIR

Dinosaurs couldn't fly – some were far too ungainly for that! The prehistoric skies were full of flying reptiles called pterosaurs. These creatures were well adapted for flight, with large wings covered with leathery skin, just like bats.

FIRST FLYERS

Rhamphorhynchus was typical of the early pterosaurs, with forward-pointing teeth for trapping insects and a long tail, which it may have used to steer with.

Rhamphorhynchus

FLYING MACHINES

As time passed, pterosaurs became more sophisticated in design. Pteranodon was the perfect flying machine. A big headcrest balanced the weight of the beak and was used as a rudder. Pteranodon flew with slow flaps of its great wings, gliding on warm air currents whenever possible.

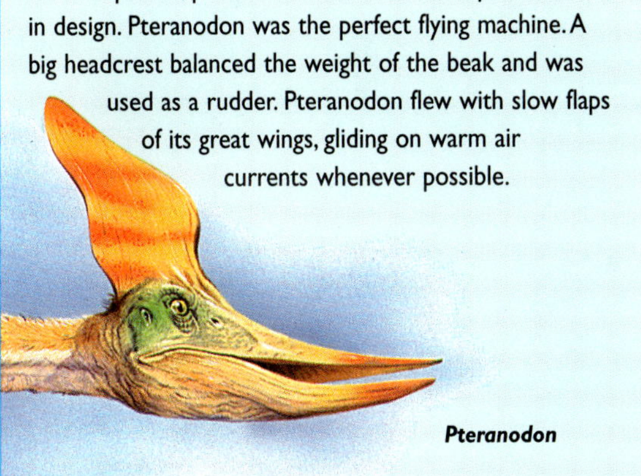

Pteranodon

DEAD GIVEAWAY

It is possible to tell what a pterosaur ate by looking at its beak.

- Dimorphodon used its sharp teeth and strong puffin-shaped beak to tear pieces of meat.

- Pterodaustro sieved small creatures out of the water with its bristly bottom jaw.

Dsungaripterus

- Dsungaripterus picked tiny animals out from cracks in the rock with its pointed beak.

GIANTS IN THE SKY

Like their reptile relatives on land and at sea, some pterosaurs grew to gigantic sizes. Quetzalcoatlus was the biggest flying animal ever, with a massive 14 m wingspan.

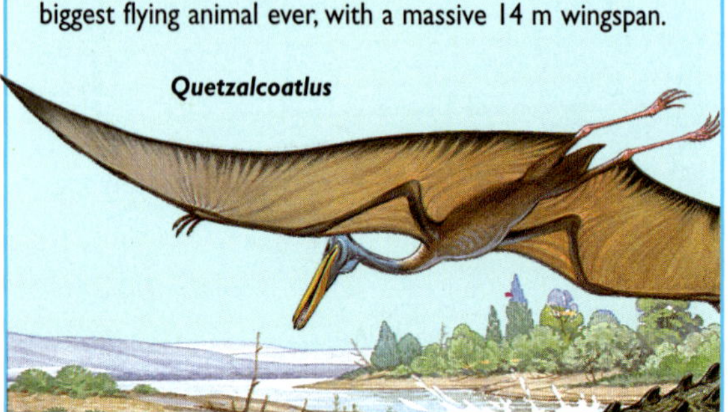

Quetzalcoatlus

BANDITS AT TWELVE O'CLOCK. BOMBS AWAY!
LES PRETEND

YEEOWCH!

TOODLE-PIP!
BAH! LES'S HEAD'S IN THE CLOUDS, AS USUAL!

DINOSAURS TODAY

Did you know there are dinosaurs in your back garden? Birds are the modern descendants of the dinosaurs. The first known bird developed from a small two-legged dinosaur in the Jurassic Period. This bird is called Archaeopteryx, which means 'ancient wing'.

BIRD OR DINOSAUR?

Archaeopteryx was a cross between a bird and a dinosaur, with both bird and reptile features. Like a bird, Archaeopteryx had feathery wings and a wishbone, but it had teeth and a bony tail like a reptile. Its skeleton is very similar to that of Compsognathus, the smallest dinosaur.

Archaeopteryx

Heron

OLD BIRDS

After Archaeopteryx, many different birds developed. Herons, ducks and owls all lived alongside dinosaurs in the Cretaceous Period.

Owl

Crocodile

THE OLDEST REPTILES

Don't confuse crocodiles with dinosaurs. Crocodiles were around in the dinosaur age, and shared the same ancestor as the dinosaurs, but they developed in a different way. They outlived their dinosaur cousins, and are now some of the oldest reptiles in the world.

MODERN MONSTERS

Some people believe that giant sea reptiles did not die out with the dinosaurs, but are still around today, hiding in deep lakes such as Loch Ness in Scotland. What do you think – could a prehistoric monster like Osteolepsis still be swimming around today?!

Osteolepsis

BILLY, WE'D BETTER GO OR WE'RE GOING TO BE EXTINCT TOO.
HERE WE GO. RIGHT WAY ROUND THIS TIME.
65M

AH, THERE'S NO TIME LIKE HOME AND NO PLACE LIKE THE PRESENT. YOU CAN STOP NOW, BILLY.
PRESENT DAY

PAWS OFF, GNASHER. IT'S MY OLD PAL.
HE'S JUST AN OLD FOSSIL NOW.

UH-OH! SPEAKING OF OLD FOSSILS . . .

COME BACK! DON'T YOU WANT TO SEE MY SLIDES OF THE JURASSIC PERIOD?
SLIDES